D is for Dala Horse

A Nordic Countries Alphabet

Written by Kathy-jo Wargin and Illustrated by Renée Graef

This book is dedicated to the Winjum (Vinjum) family
who immigrated to Minnesota from Aurland, Norway,
and to the Nelson family who immigrated to Minnesota from Trondheim, Norway.
Thank you for your resilience and your dream.

—K. J. W.

To my mom and Rhonda

—R. G.

We gratefully acknowledge the expertise and assistance of Carl Klintborg, Håkan Carlsson, and the staff at the American
Swedish Institute. The ASI is a historic mansion, museum, and cultural center that serves as a gathering place for people to share stories
and experiences around universal themes of tradition, migration, craft, and the arts, all informed by enduring ties to Sweden.
Visit them in Minneapolis, Minnesota, or at www.americanswedishinst.org to learn more and share your story.

Sleeping Bear Press™

2395 South Huron Parkway, Suite 200, Ann Arbor, MI 48104
www.sleepingbearpress.com

Printed and bound in the United States.

10 9 8 7 6

Library of Congress Cataloging-in-Publication Data

Wargin, Kathy-jo.
D is for dala horse : a Nordic countries alphabet /
written by Kathy-jo Wargin ; illustrated by Renee Graef.
p. cm.
ISBN 978-1-58536-510-4
1. Scandinavia—Juvenile literature. 2. Alphabet books—Juvenile literature.
I. Graef, Renee, ill. II. Title.
DL5.W37 2010
948—dc22
2010011857

Greenland

Svalbard

Iceland

Sweden

Faroe Islands

Finland

Norway

Åland

Denmark

Nordic Countries

The arctic fox is a native species of Arctic regions in the Northern Hemisphere. This small mammal is well suited for the extreme frigid conditions of the Arctic climate. Its dense, furry coat helps it retain a comfortable body temperature. Its keen sense of hearing helps it detect prey beneath the snow of the arctic land. The coat of the arctic fox, which is white in winter, turns brown in the summer.

The Arctic Circle is an imaginary circle located approximately 66.5 degrees north of the equator. Within this circle is the southern limit of the area where the sun does not set on the day of the summer solstice, or rise on the day of the winter solstice. A is also for Archipelago, a group of large and small islands. The Stockholm Archipelago is a group of approximately 90,000 islands off the coast of Sweden.

Far north in the **A**rctic Circle,
land of midnight sun,
the color-changing **A**rctic Fox
is always on the run.

B is for my **B**unad,
a Norwegian way to dress
wear a pretty sash and shawl,
or a handsome vest.

The *bunad* is the traditional folk costume of Norway. Every Nordic country has its own version of a folk costume, which usually consists of an ensemble with ornate embroidery, shawls, blouses, and jewelry of silver or gold. The traditional folk costume is meant to represent different regions of Scandinavia and is representative of folk and peasant life. Today such attire is worn for many occasions and galas. In Norway a traditional bunad for a male includes a vest or waistcoat with short trousers.

B is also for Baltic Sea. The Baltic Sea is an arm of the Atlantic Ocean and is located in northern Europe. The Baltic Sea is edged by the countries of Denmark, Sweden, Finland, Estonia, Latvia, Lithuania, Poland, Russia, and Germany.

B b

Copenhagen is the largest city of Denmark and also its capital. Established in the tenth century as a fishing village and harbor, it was named the capital of Denmark in the fifteenth century. The original name for the city was Køpmannæhafn, meaning "merchant's harbor." Copenhagen is located on the eastern shore of the island of Zealand as well as partially on the island of Amager. Its harbor faces Oresund, the waterway that separates Denmark from Sweden. Denmark is rich in culture, design, architecture, and progressive in its environmental policies. Denmark is the oldest constitutional monarchy in Scandinavia.

C is also for Crayfish Party. In Sweden, it is popular to hold a crayfish party in August. Crayfish are often served cold and with dill seasoning, and the parties are a festive event held outdoors with paper lanterns and decorations.

The capital of Denmark
Cis a lively place to be.
Copenhagen is on a harbor
that was settled near the sea.

Here's a bright red **D**ala horse,
hand-painted with our pleasure.
This symbol of our friendship
is a gift we hope you treasure!

The Dalecarlian Horse is known to most as the Dala horse and has become a highly recognizable worldwide symbol of Sweden. The original carvings were made in the Dalarna region when forest workers carved little horses for their children. In the 1800s, people began to embellish the horses by hand-painting them in traditional Dalarna patterns. Today most Dala horses are still carved and painted by hand, making each small wooden statue a one-of-a-kind piece of folk art.

D d

Everyman's right begins with E—
a promise to let every person walk free.

In the countries of Norway, Iceland, Sweden, and Finland, an ancient way of life is the right to roam, which means access for everyone. This privilege is called Everyman's Right and it allows people general access to walk, ski, cycle, or camp freely on public and private lands in the countryside, as long as it is not in direct vicinity of a person's home or garden, and as long as it causes no damage to the land. Each country may have small variances in their application of Everyman's Right, but in all countries it is understood that with this privilege comes the responsibility to be good stewards of the land.

E is also for two famous Edvards. Edvard Grieg was born in Bergen, Norway in 1843. He is best known for his Piano Concerto in A Minor as well as the music he composed for Henrik Ibsen's play *Peer Gynt*. Edvard Munch was a Norwegian painter and printmaker born in 1863 in Loten, Norway. He Is most well known for his painting titled *The Scream*, which is part of a series called The Frieze of Life.

Ee

The Republic of Finland is the eighth largest country in the European Union and yet one of the most sparsely populated. The largest concentration of people reside in the capital city of Helsinki. As a region comprised of lakes, forests, and islands, it is also home to Lake Saimaa, the fourth largest lake in Europe and home to the endangered Saimaa ringed seal. The Kalevala is the national epic of Finland. Compiled by Elias Lonnrot from Finnish and Karelian folklore, the poem has more than 22,000 verses and celebrates the history of the region.

Fjords were created when glaciers made deep abrasions into the bedrock resulting in long, narrow inlets with very steep sides. Although fjords and other similar glacial features can be found throughout the world, the two longest fjords are found in Scandinavia. The longest is the Scoresby Sund in Greenland, followed by the Sognefjord in Norway.

Ff

Do you see the Fjords? Each one came to be
when carved by the glaciers and filled by the sea.

We like to go Fishing, it's our way to eat.
Food from the sea is a good Nordic treat.

F is for Finland,
blue lakes and white snow.
Our poem The Kalevala,
is the epic to know.

KALEVALA

Geographically speaking, the country of Greenland belongs to North America. It is the world's largest island and an autonomous country within the Kingdom of Denmark. More than 80 percent of Greenland is covered by an ice cap called the Greenlandic Ice Sheet. As the least populated country in the world, it is believed to have been settled when Erik the Red arrived with Vikings, who named it Greenland in the hope of making it sound attractive to others. Greenland is home to the white polar bear, walrus, and musk-ox, as well as whales, narwhals, reindeer, and seals. Summer is brief and intense, prompting a wide array of flowering plants and grasses that cover the land providing a contrast in colors.

G g

The island of Greenland has glaciers to view,
with mountains and whales, white polar bears, too.

Many well-known fairy tales, such as *The Ugly Duckling, The Emperor's New Clothes, Thumbelina,* and *The Little Mermaid* were written by Hans Christian Andersen, who was born in Odense, Denmark in 1805. His first collection of fairy tales was published in 1835, with two additional volumes following in 1836 and 1837. Hans Christian Andersen died in 1875 near Copenhagen. A statue of The Little Mermaid, unveiled in 1913, stands on a rock in Copenhagen's harbor, serving as a major attraction for tourists and fans of the author.

Hh

Hans Christian Andersen, we all know his name.
He gave the world stories and brought Denmark fame.

The Republic of Iceland is a volcanically active island in the North Atlantic Ocean. Its terrain is diverse. You will find mountains and glaciers, sandy fields, and rivers flowing to the sea. Settlement began in 874 with its first permanent Norwegian settler, named Ingólfur Arnarson. As the centuries followed, so did more Nordic peoples, and today the culture of Iceland is based upon this Norse heritage. Iceland is famous for its Icelandic Sagas, stories believed to have been written in the 13th and 14th centuries. The sagas are histories of events that took place between the Norse and Celtic inhabitants of Iceland in the 10th and early 11th centuries. The capital of Iceland is Reykjavik, which is in southwestern Iceland.

The Republic of Iceland,
  the land of the Norse,
is famous for sagas
  and geysers of force.

Jokkmokk is a community in northern Sweden. It is north of the Arctic Circle, and its name in Sami language means "bend in the river." The Sami are an indigenous people of northern Europe. For more than 400 years, the Sami people of northern Scandinavia have been meeting here each winter to trade goods and share stories. Established by King Karl IX of Sweden as a way to influence trade and commerce, the market today is a lively and entertaining place to visit, attracting people from all over the world.

The great Jokkmokk market
is busy each year.
It's Sami tradition
to meet and trade here.

J j

Norway, Denmark, and Sweden are known as kingdoms, but each differs slightly from the other. The Kingdom of Norway is a constitutional monarchy, which means the hereditary king acts as head of state. The duties of this king are ceremonial in nature. The elected bodies of the country are the ones that hold the powers of the legislative and executive branches. The Kingdom of Denmark is also a constitutional monarchy and hereditary by nature. Acting as head of state, this monarch cannot independently perform political acts but can participate in the formation of new government. The Kingdom of Sweden is also based upon a hereditary monarchy, and the title was passed to the eldest male until the 1979 Act of Succession that changed the rule to allow the role to be passed to the firstborn, whether male or female.

K k

Norway, Denmark, Sweden, too
are fit with heads of state.
This makes each a **K**ingdom
and a monarchy by fate.

And **K** is for our money.
It's fun to spend through town.
The krona and the krone,
both of which mean crown.

Tasty little Lingonberries,
jam and sauce to try.
Can you smell the Lutefisk?
It's fish that's soaked in lye.

The lingonberry is a small evergreen shrub. As a member of the flowering plant family, it bears fruit that is easily harvested. The tart berries are easy to cook and can also be mashed. Most often they are sweetened and made into jams, sauces, or compotes. A favorite Scandinavian dish is meatballs and potatoes with lingonberry preserves. Lutefisk, which means "lye-fish," is whitefish or cod soaked in lye over the course of several days, which can give it a very strong odor when cooked. It is a traditional dish of the Nordic countries, and commonly eaten on Christmas whether in Scandinavia or in homes of Scandinavian-Americans.

L l

Midsummer is the celebration of the summer solstice, and it is one of Sweden's most important holidays. It is celebrated in mid-June with traditional Swedish events such as collecting greens and flowers to decorate the midsummer pole before raising it. When the pole is raised, friends and families dance around it singing folksongs and listening to traditional music. The holiday is filled with good foods such as pickled herring, potatoes, and drink. In Norway and Denmark it is celebrated on June 23 with bonfires and songs. In Finland it is celebrated on a Saturday between June 20 and 26 with midsummer poles, bonfires, music, and taking saunas in the evening.

We love the Midsummer folksongs and cheer
to bring us together
the best time of year!

The term Nordic countries identifies the Nordic region of Northern Europe and North America. It includes the countries Sweden, Norway, Finland, Denmark, Iceland, and their associated territories of Greenland, the Faroe Islands, Svalbard, and Aland. The countries cooperate politically in a Nordic Council and share a population of approximately 25 million people.

Alfred Nobel, the inventor of dynamite, was born in Stockholm, Sweden. When he died in Italy, he left his fortune for the establishment of the Nobel Prizes, and every year we honor those people who have made the greatest contributions to literature, science, medicine, and peace.

Let's name the Nordic lands
in a list to share with you:
Sweden, Norway, Denmark,
Finland, and Iceland, too.

And N is for the Nobel Prize
A good way to remind
that we should try to live in peace
and serve all humankind.

N n

ALFR. NOBEL

NAY
MDCCC
XXXIII
OB
MDCCC
XCVI

Oslo is the capital of Norway and also its largest city. With a population of nearly 1.5 million people, Oslo sits at the northernmost end of the Oslofjord. Founded in the year 1048 by King Harald III of Norway, the city was nearly lost to a fire in 1624. When it was rebuilt, it was renamed Christiania. Effective January 1, 1925, the name was restored to Oslo. Oslo is often referred to as the "City of Tigers" related to a reference by author Bjørnstjerne Bjørnson in 1870, although there are no tigers in Norway. The reference was related to the author's perception of Oslo as a cold and dangerous place. Today Oslo is a thriving metropolitan city.

At the head of the fjord is a sight to behold—
O is for Oslo, one thousand years old.

Sweet little Puffins, a coastal affair.
They rest on the cliffs and they float through the air.

The puffin is a species of auk and is a seabird that hunts fish by diving into the water. The puffins of Scandinavia are Atlantic puffins, and they form colonies on coasts and islands. The Atlantic puffin is nicknamed the clown of the sea because of its comical appearance. Most of the world's puffins are found in Iceland, where 60 percent of the population breed, and they also are commonly found on the Faroe Islands. Puffins are easily identified by their black and white coats and orange legs and beaks.

P p

A polar night is 24 hours of darkness or twilight that happens inside the polar circle. There are also times of prolonged twilight during the winter months, and during this time the land is covered with snow and can reflect the stars and the moon, giving the landscape a quiet, subdued feeling. The polar regions are perfectly suited for northern lights, or aurora borealis, which is a natural light display resulting from the interaction between the earth's magnetic field and solar wind as electrons collide with oxygen and nitrogen atoms. You can observe northern lights in autumn, winter, and early spring, and they most commonly happen between the early evening and early morning hours.

It gets very Quiet as polar nights fall.
When northern lights dance, it is peaceful for all.

Runestones were raised with a story engraved
to teach us of Vikings and how they behaved.

RWe love our **R**eindeer that live freely here.
Rosemaling is painting, an art we hold dear.

Most runestones are from the Viking Age and are found in Scandinavia. A runestone is most commonly a raised stone with runic writing inscribed upon it. Most often, runestones were erected as a way to offer a memorial for the deceased, to mark territory, or to express details about an important event. Although most runestones are found in Denmark, Sweden, and Norway, many runestones have been discovered in other countries, offering clues to the patterns of Viking exploration. Runestones were typically painted a bright color when erected; however, you will find that in most runestones, the color has worn away due to age.

Although domesticated reindeer can be found throughout the northern region of Scandinavia and Iceland, the last remaining wild reindeer of Europe are found only in the mountainous region of southern Norway. This wild reindeer has a short, wiry gray-brown coat, and both males and females will grow antlers.

Rosemaling simply means "rose painting" and is a traditional folk art of Norway. There are three main styles of rosemaling, each named for the region of Norway in which it originated—they are Telemark, Hallingdal, and Rogaland.

Rr

On December 13, Scandinavia celebrates Saint Lucia, also known as the patron saint of light. Although generally associated with Sweden, Saint Lucia is celebrated throughout the other countries as well where people often awaken to the eldest female child dressed in a white robe or gown and wearing a crown of candles while offering Lucia buns or treats with a warm beverage.

Christmas in Scandinavia most often includes a Christmas Smorgasbord referred to as the julbord. Smorgasbord is a Swedish word. *Smorgas* means open face sandwich, and *bord* means table. The smorgasbord refers to a table of food, typically a wide variety of dishes, usually both hot and cold, served to a group of people in the manner of a serve-yourself buffet. In Norway it is referred to as koldtbord, and in Denmark it is a kolde bord.

Scandinavia is a commonly known term for the kingdoms of Sweden, Norway, and Denmark, and is derived from the geographic region known as the Scandinavian Peninsula. Casually, the countries of Finland, Iceland, Greenland, and the Faroe Islands have been included in the term Scandinavia. However, these countries are not geographically part of the Scandinavian Peninsula but do share the same history and culture. To reflect this, the term Nordic countries is used to officially define the countries as a collective.

S s

S
In mid December you will find
in Saint Lucia's light,
    a greeting in the morning
        by a girl dressed in white.

Then as Christmas does arrive
        we have tasty things to eat—
a Smorgasbord of favorites,
tradition and a treat.

Trolls are common in Norse mythology. They are often portrayed as cruel, trickster creatures appearing in giant form with large facial features who live in the hills, woodlands, or deep forests of Scandinavia. Tomtens, also known as nisse, are also mythical characters in Scandinavian folklore, but appear as small gnome-like creatures, sometimes in the form of an old fellow who takes care of children and animals, or helps farmers with their chores. The Finnish equivalent is the tonttu.

Tt

Throughout this land of Nordic myths
wherever you may stroll
hidden in the forest Tomtens or a Troll.
could be

Uppsala University is the oldest institution of higher education in all of the Nordic countries. Established in 1477 by Archbishop Jakob Ulvsson of Uppsala with no more than 50 students, today the university is a large, diverse institution. Renowned figures from Uppsala's past include Anders Celsius, inventor of the Celsius scale, botanist Carolus Linnaeus who developed a new way for us to categorize plants, Olof Rudbeck, who discovered the lymphatic system and its effects on the body, historian Erik Gustaf Geijer, and eight Nobel laureates throughout the years. Today Uppsala is a prominent research university and known throughout the world.

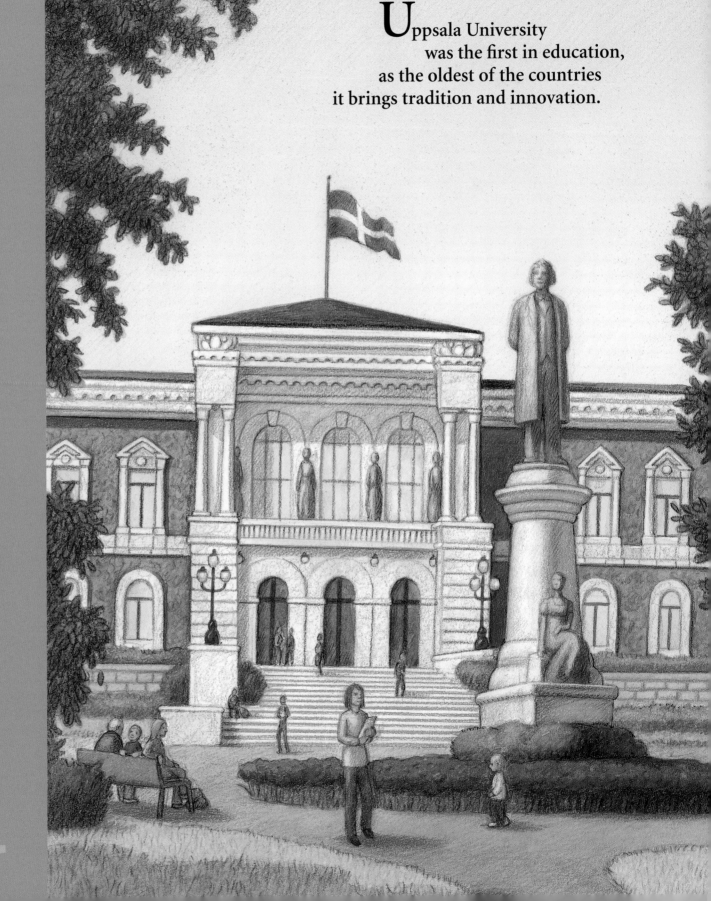

Uppsala University
was the first in education,
as the oldest of the countries
it brings tradition and innovation.

Trader, warrior, merchants too, the **V**ikings on their ships
traveled out across the seas in many Viking trips.

Vikings were also known as Norsemen, and from the late eighth to the early eleventh centuries, they raided and colonized many areas of Europe, traveling in ships. One such type of vessel used by the Vikings was known as a longship. Its long and narrow design was specifically suited for exploration and warfare. Another Viking vessel was the knarr, a merchant ship designed to carry cargo. While the exploits of the Vikings are the subject of much discussion and debate, they were known as explorers and merchants as well as raiders and pirates. The Viking Age is an integral part of medieval history in many parts of the world.

V is also for Vasa. The Vasa was a Swedish warship that sank on her maiden voyage in 1628. In the 1960s, her mostly intact hull was salvaged, and today the ship resides in the Vasa Museum in Stockholm and is a widely visited tourist attraction.

V
v

Although winter in the Nordic countries usually means short days and long nights, it also means snow and snowy outdoor activities. Scandinavian culture has always been associated with love of nature, the outdoors, and winter activity. You will find people busy with cross-country and downhill skiing, ski jumping, sledding, dogsledding, hiking, skating, snowshoeing, and skijoring, which is the popular sport of cross-country skiing with your dog in a harness.

Welcome to the **W**inter
with a white and snowy view.
The outdoors is a wonderland
and filled with much to do.

W
W

The word ski comes from an Old Norse word *skíð*, which means a stick of wood. The word ski is used throughout the world today to identify this common winter sport, although in Norway, no verb equivalent such as the word "skiing" exists as it does in other languages. There are several famous ski races in Scandinavia, such as Sweden's Vasaloppet, and the Birkebeiner, which takes place in Norway.

It's said that we are born on skis.
We strap them on and go.
X is for cross-country sports
and tracks upon the snow.

The Nordic Cross is also known as the Scandinavian Cross and is an emblem on the flags of all the Nordic countries. The first flag to bear this design was the flag of Denmark, and the Norwegian flag was the first flag to use three colors instead of two in its design. The cross is said to represent Christianity, and although all the flags share this emblem, they each have their own histories, identities, and timelines. For instance in Finland, the white and blue colors represent the thousands of lakes and the white of the snow that covers the land each winter.

Y y

Sweden's Yellow Nordic Cross
upon a field of blue—
Do you see the other flags
with Nordic Crosses too?

The mountainous country of Norway has many zigzag roads including the road called Trollstigen, which in English means The Troll Path. This steep, turning mountain road is located in Rauma, Norway and is part of Norwegian National Road 63. With its hairpin turns and steep elevation, it is a popular route for tourists. The road is closed during the autumn and winter months.

Z z

Z is for the **Z**igzag roads
through mountains, coasts, and more.
Fjords and cities, tundras too—
there's so much to explore.

From the Arctic Circle
to the islands in the sea,
we hope you'll visit often
Nordic Countries A to Z!

Kathy-jo Wargin

Kathy-jo Wargin is the best-selling author of more than 45 books for children including Michigan's Official State Children's Book *The Legend of Sleeping Bear*. Among her many awards for her work are an International Reading Association (IRA) Children's Choice Award for *The Legend of the Loon* and an IRA Teacher's Choice Award for *Win One for the Gipper*, and a National Parenting Publications Award for *Alfred Nobel: The Man Behind the Peace Prize*. Kathy-jo was born and raised in northern Minnesota and has always been proud of her Scandinavian heritage. She is a descendant of Ole Winjum of the Winjum (Vinjum) farm in Aurland, Norway. She currently lives in Minnetonka, Minnesota with her husband, Ed Wargin, and their son, Jake. You can visit her website at www.kathy-jowargin.com.

Renée Graef

Renée Graef has illustrated more than 70 books for children. The most well known are the "Kirsten" books in the American Girl Collection and the "My First Little House" books by Laura Ingalls Wilder. In addition to *D is for Dala Horse*, Renée also illustrated *A Girl Named Dan*, *B is for Bookworm: A Library Alphabet*, *Paul Bunyan's Sweetheart*, and *B is for Badger: A Wisconsin Alphabet*. Renée lives in Cedarburg, Wisconsin with her family.